How Many F

by Anne Diorio

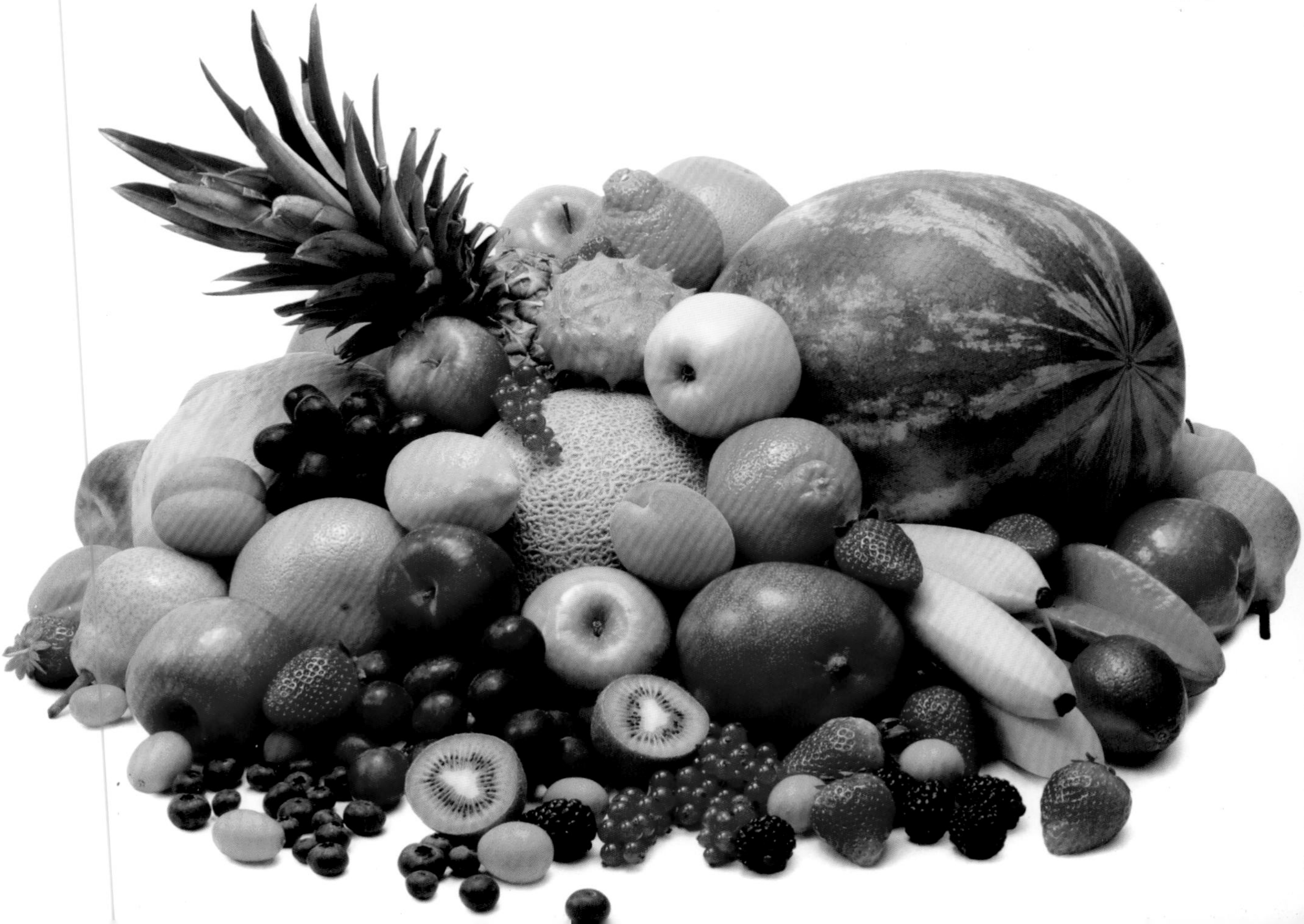

I have 1 watermelon.

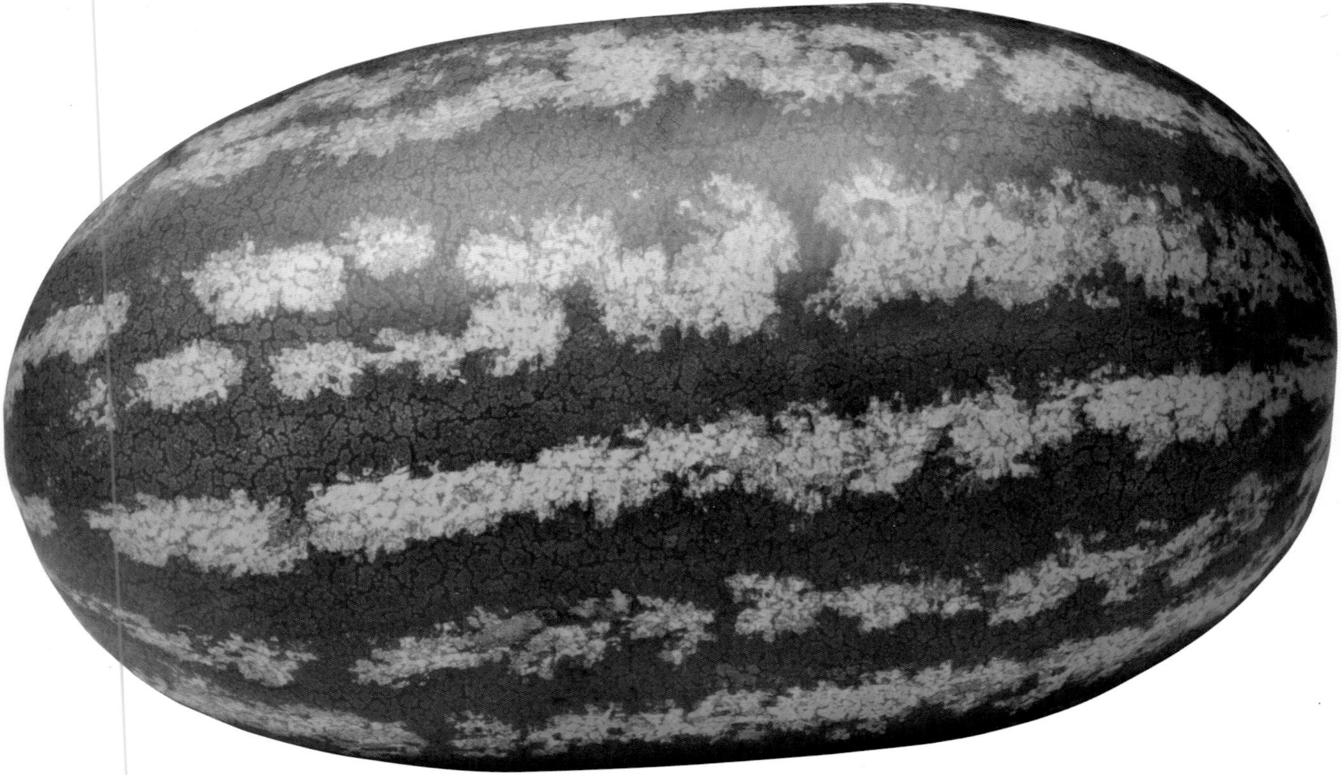

I have 2 bananas.

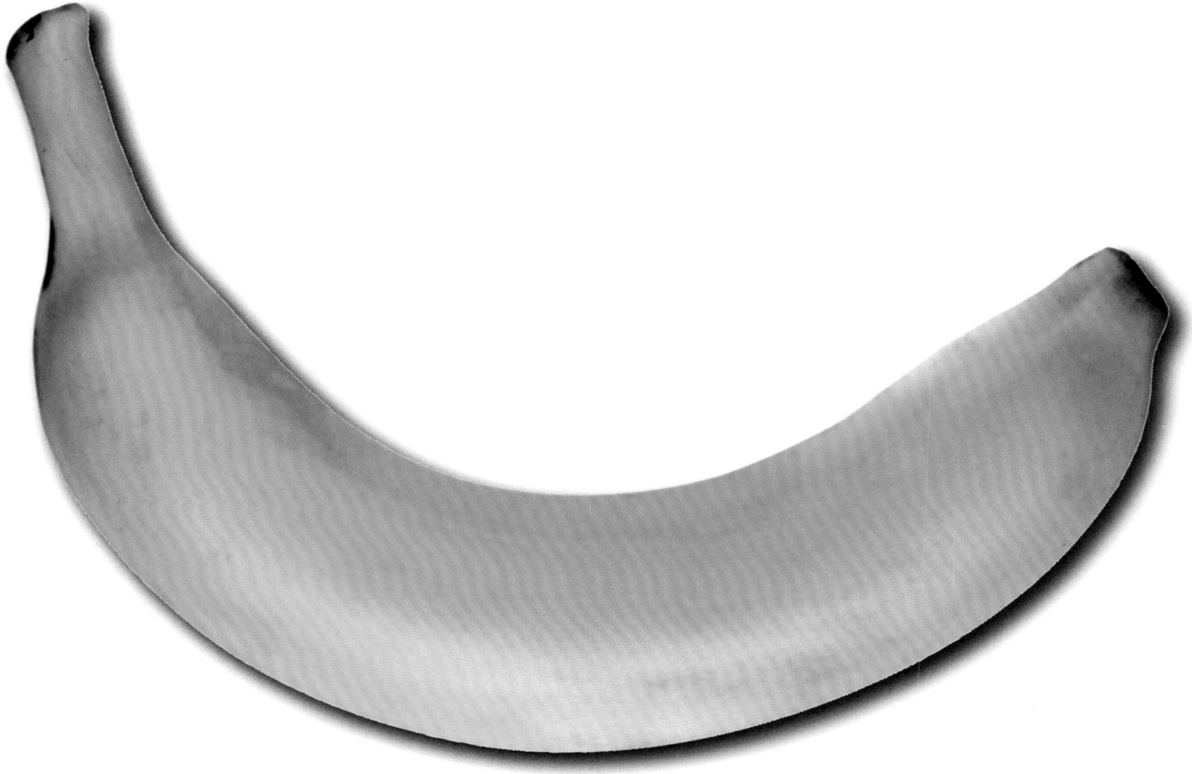

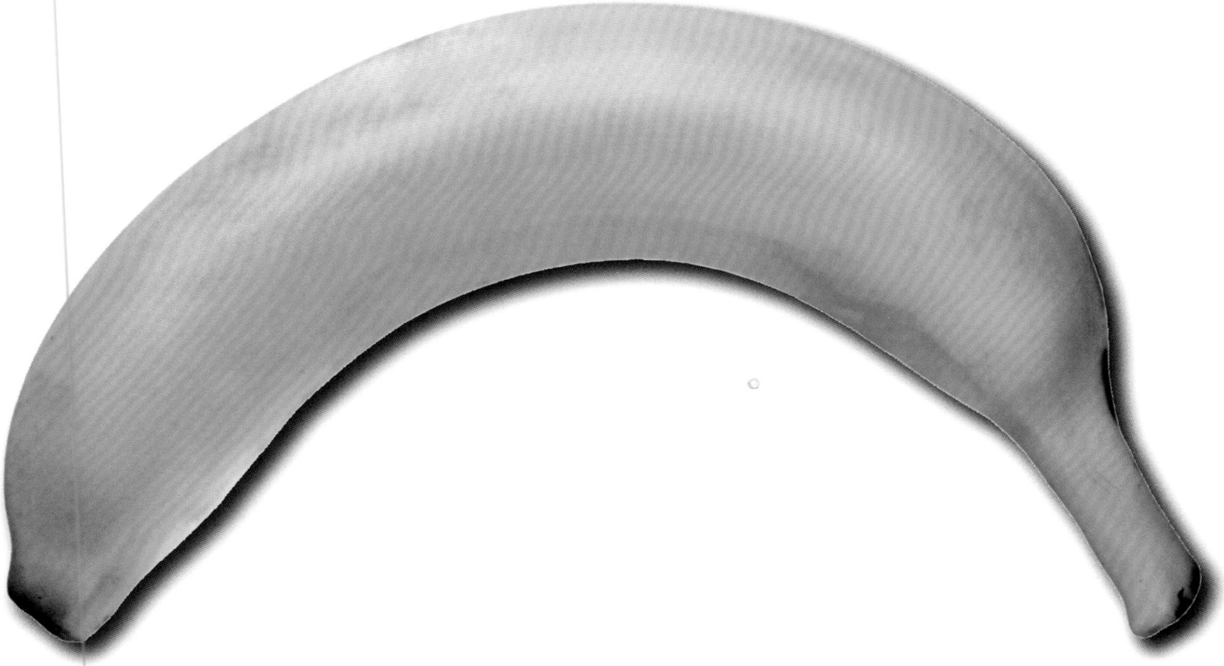

I have 3 oranges.

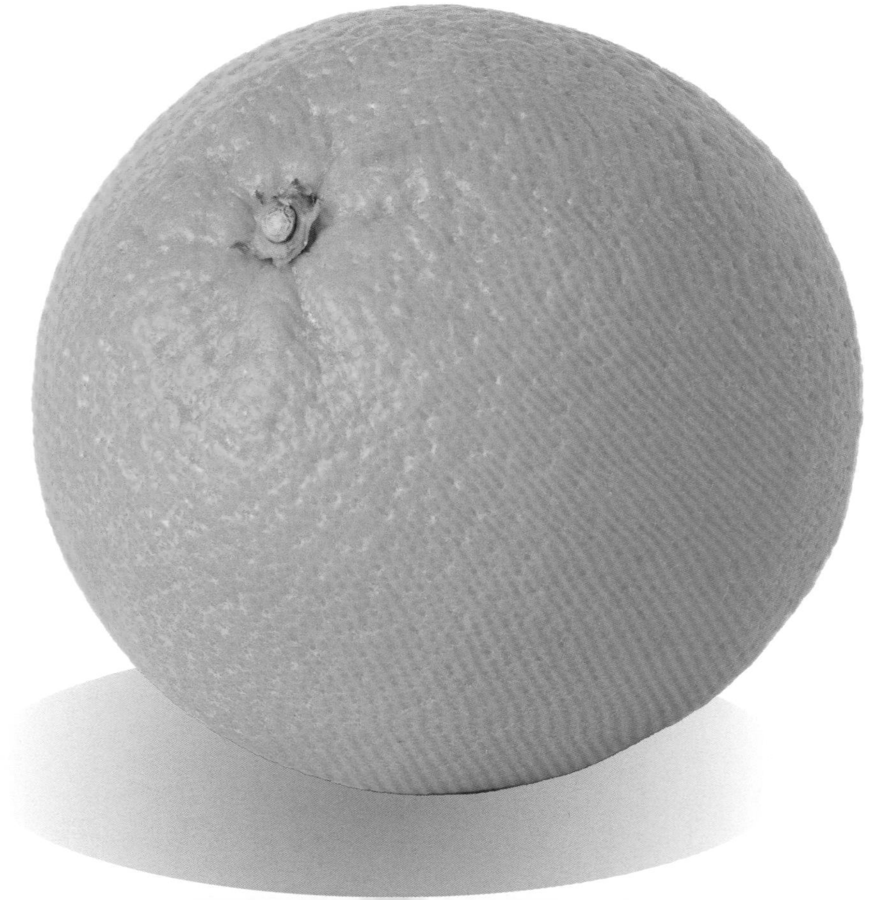

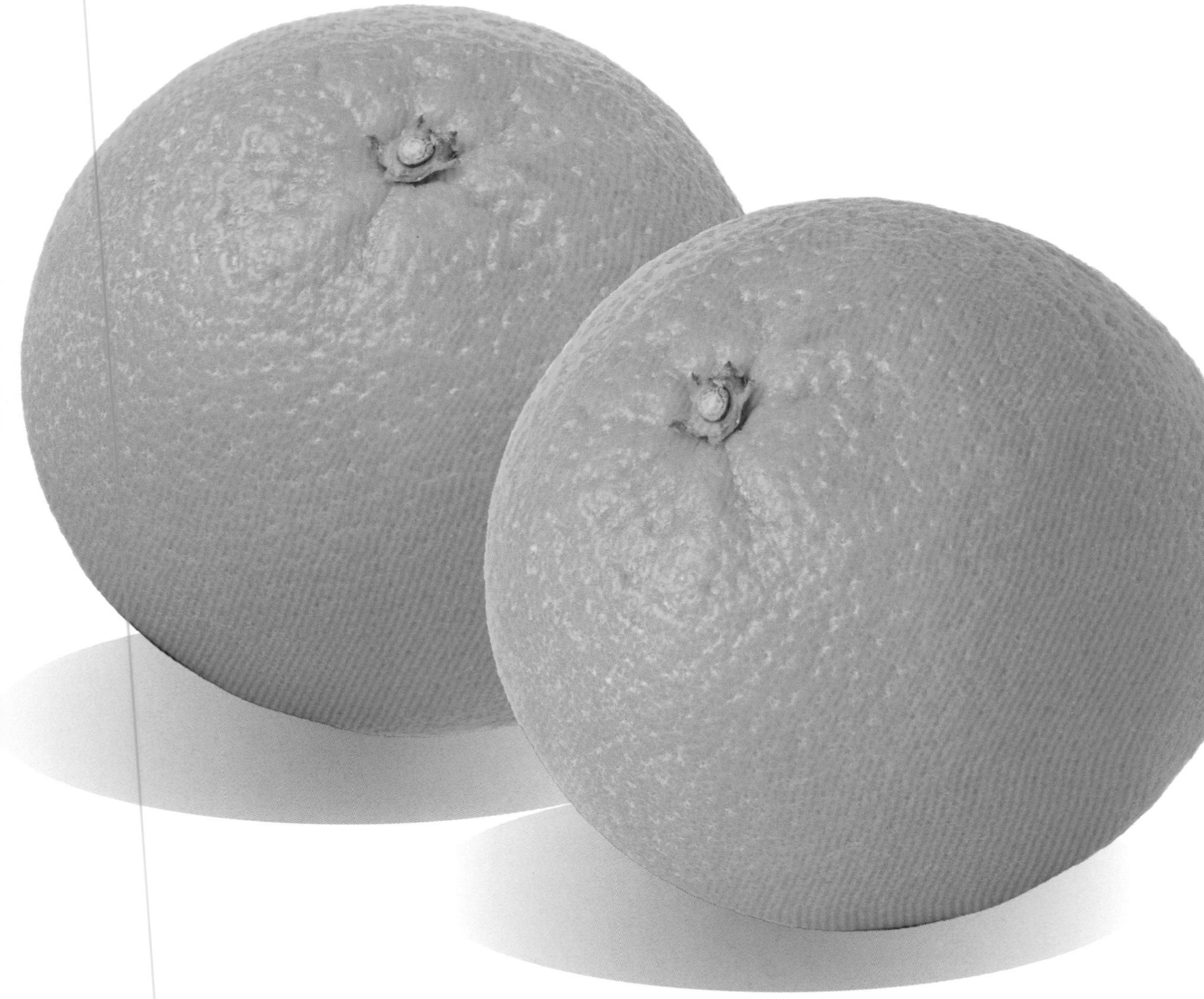

I have 4 apples.

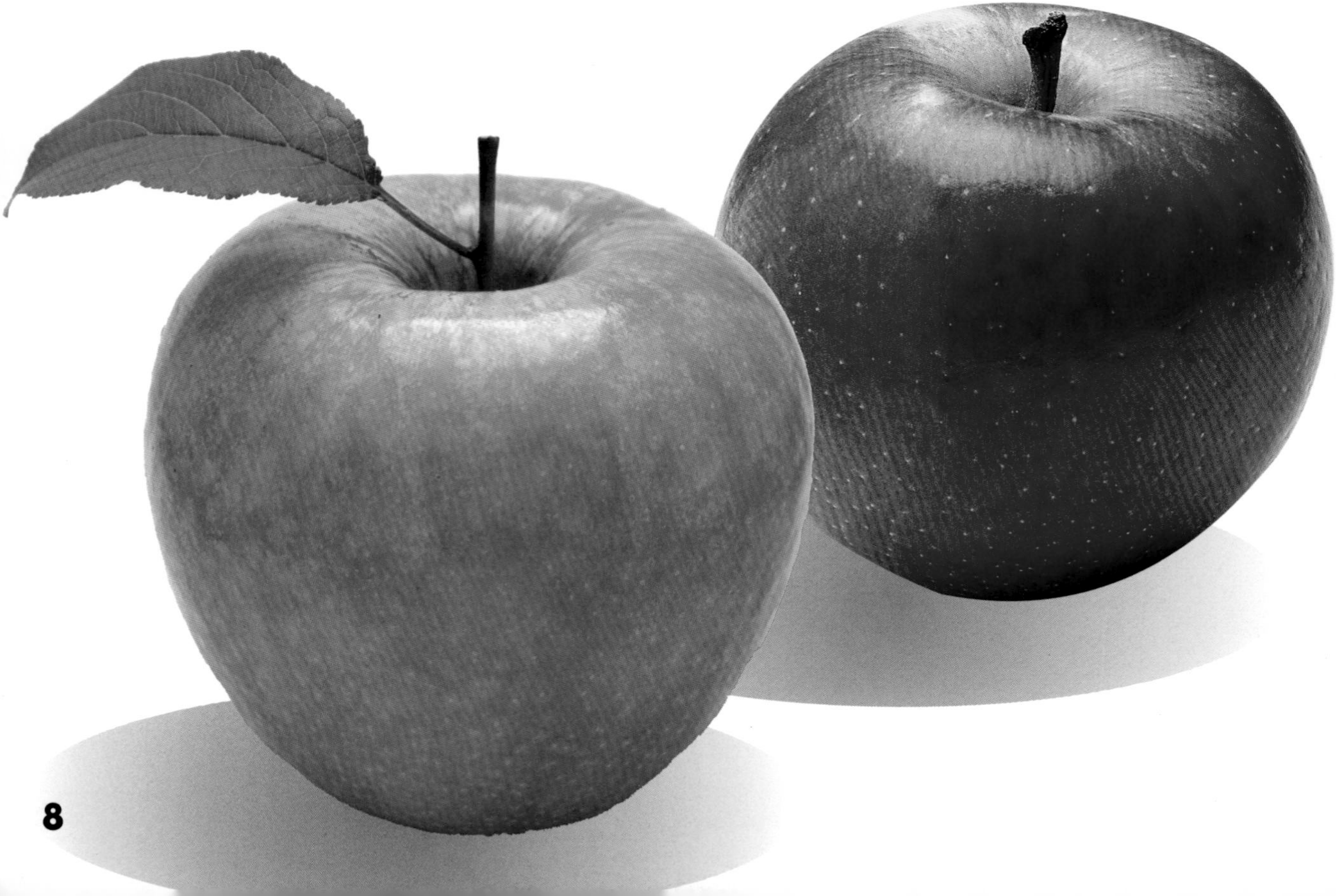

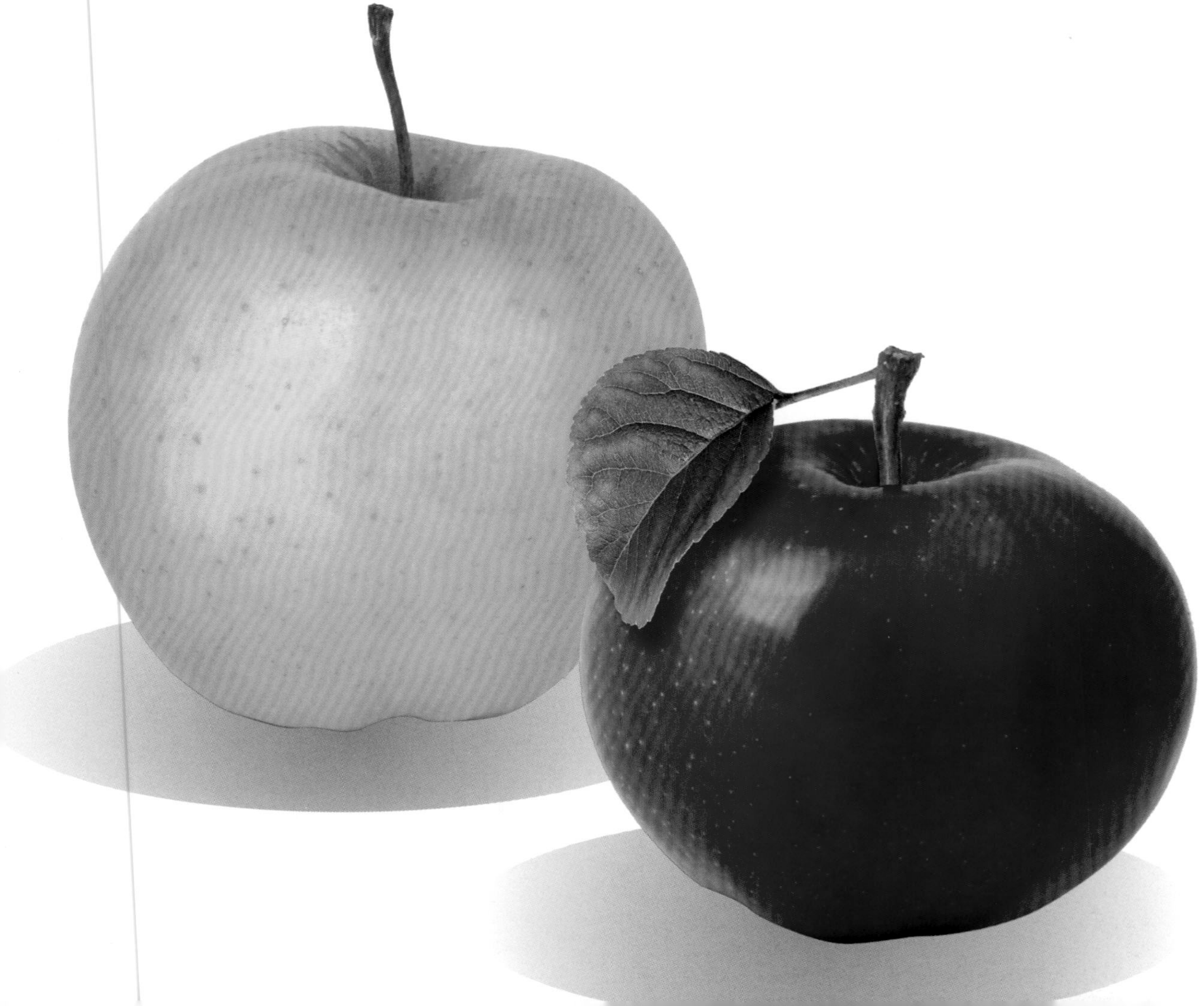

I have 5 pears.

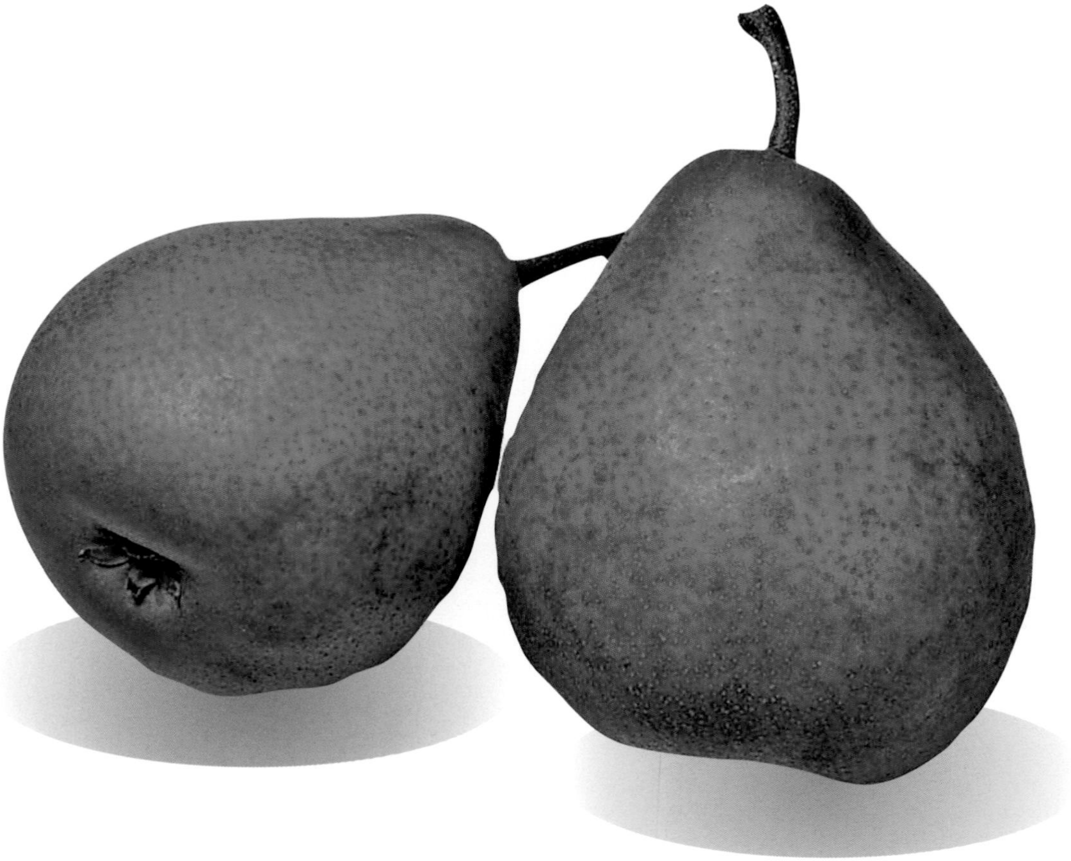

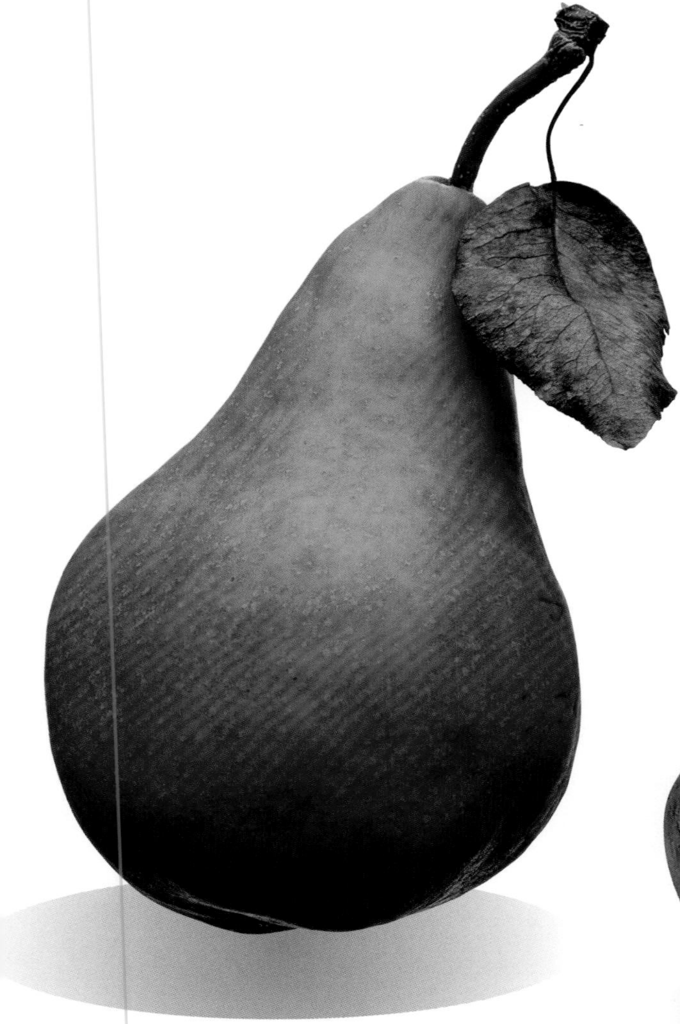

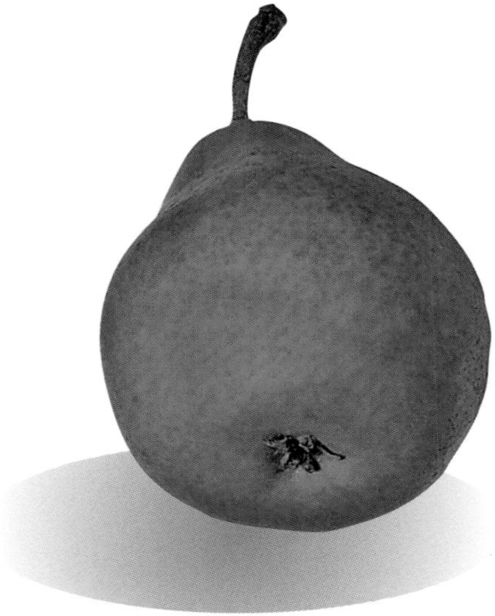

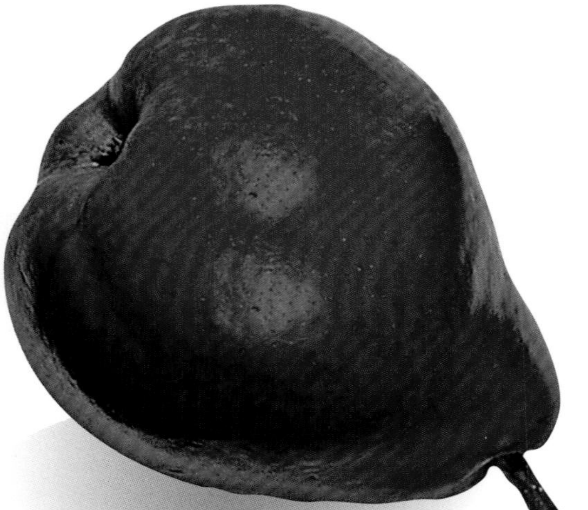

I have 6 strawberries.

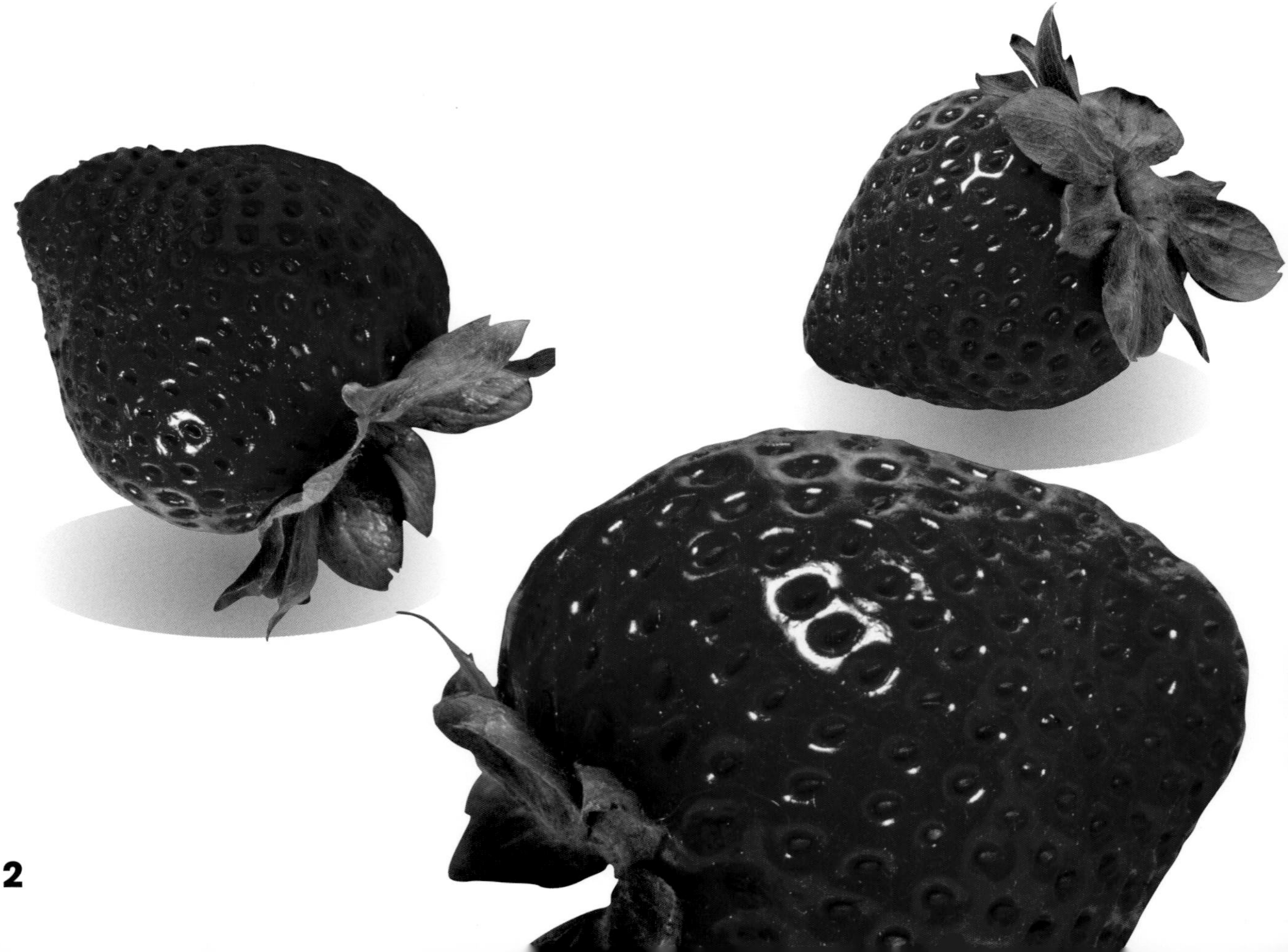

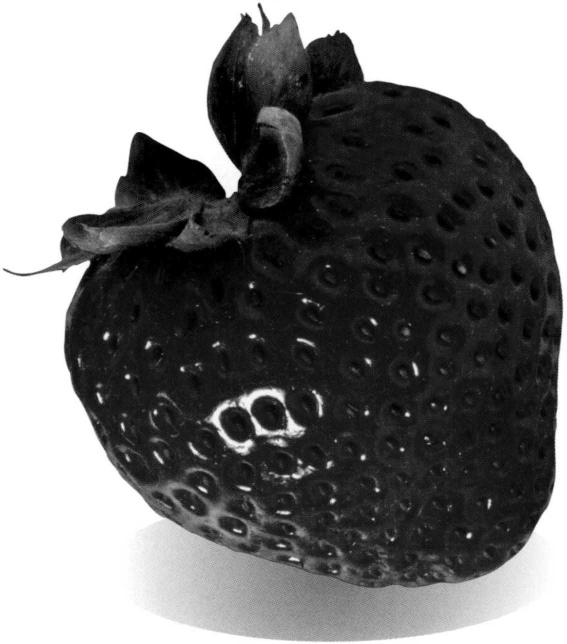
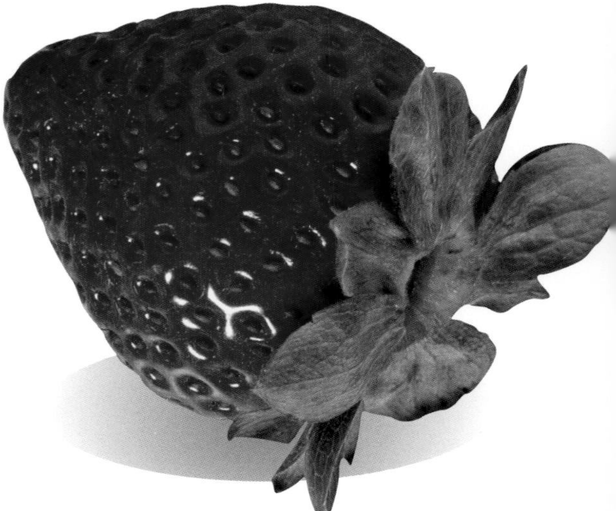
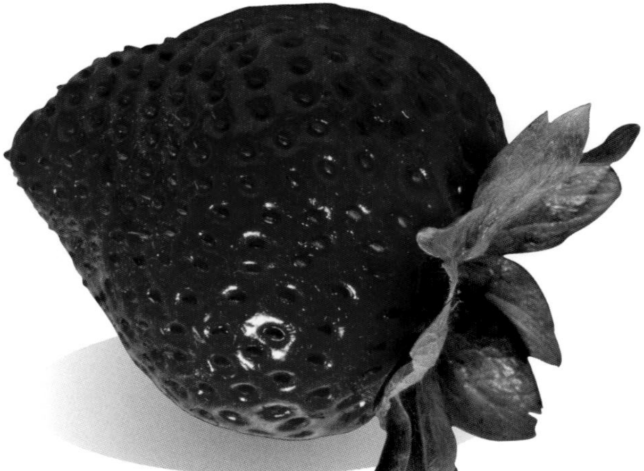

I have 7 grapes.

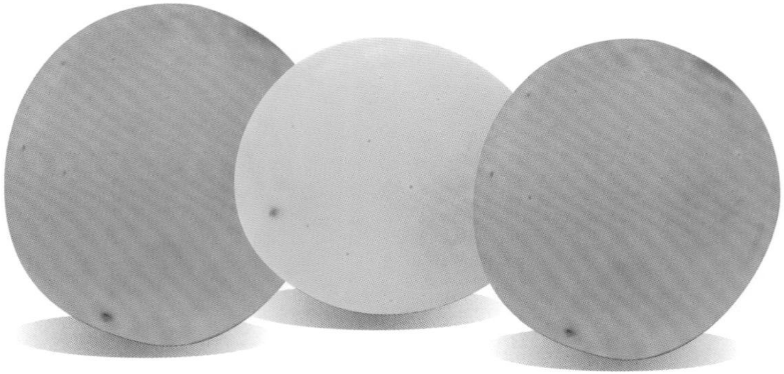

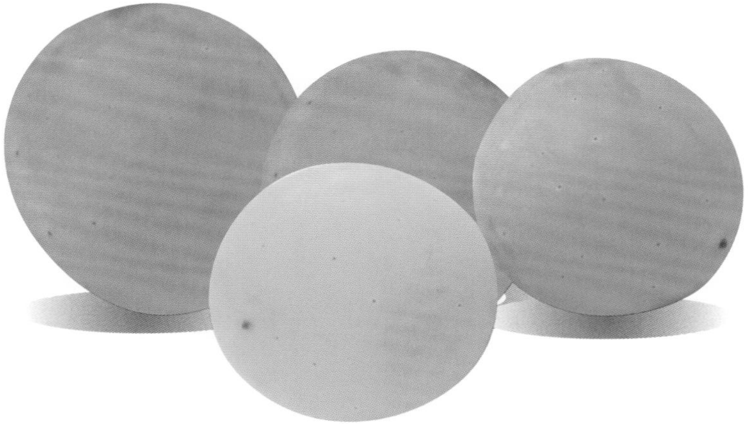

How many lemons do I have?

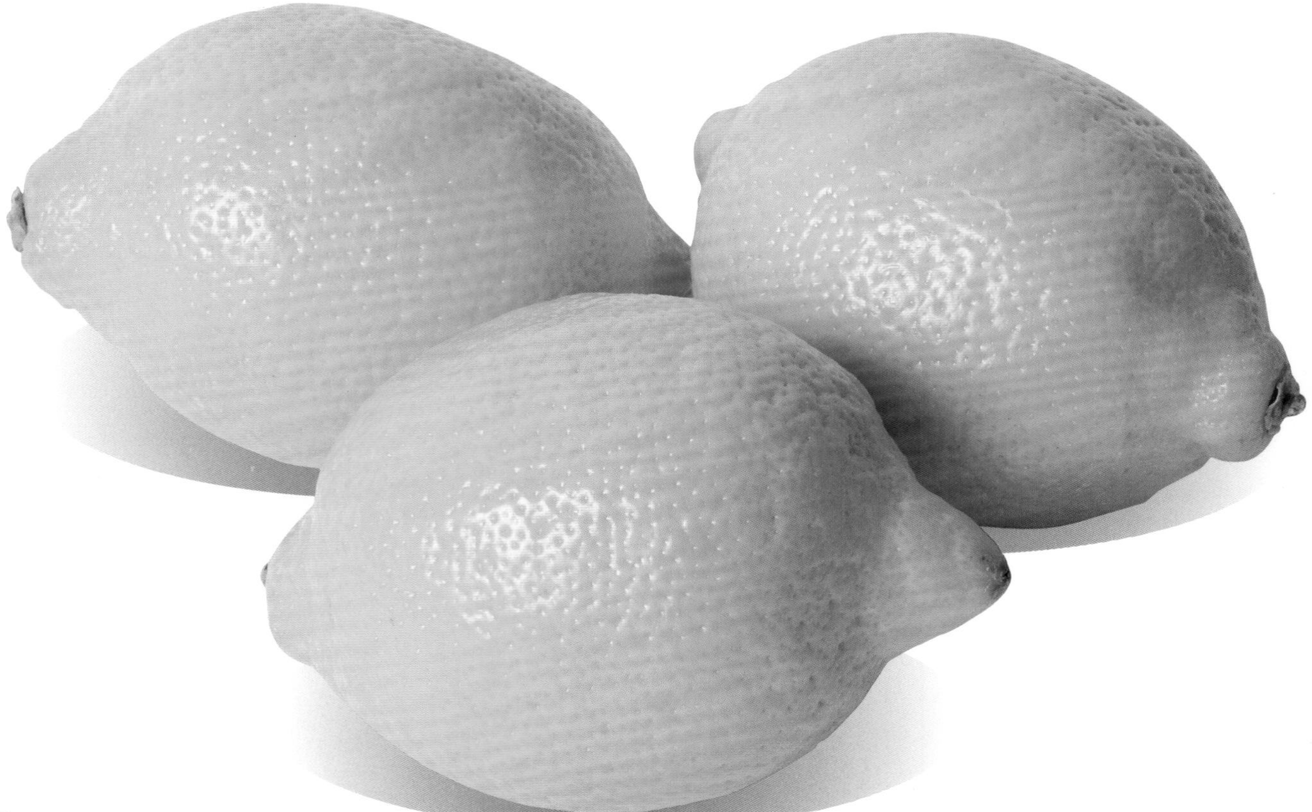